by Frank Smith

orthrop's

-38A / AT-38 / T-38C TALON   uncovered by Willy Peeters

One of the sleekest and most elegant aircraft ever to grace the skies is the Northrop T-38 Talon. people will contradict that. Not the thousands of student pilots who graduated on this gracious jet to beco highly skilled fighter pilots, nor the instructors who initiated them in what for many would be their first experience. Especially not the USAF Thunderbirds who, in the seventies, choose the Talon as their designa performance platform, amazing crowds all over the world. The first ATC (Air Training Command) T-38 delivered to Randolph AFB in Texas on March 17,1961, where a lot of the pictures in this book were tak While over there I was informed of the intended upgrade of the T-38 which was under way, all of which can read in the second chapter of this book.

Despite its popularity not many books have been published on the T-38, especially not from a model viewpoint. Rather than using the pages of this book to describe the development and operations of the T we filled them with pictures of the aircraft itself. If you like to know more about the history and deploym of the Talon, we can highly recommend a book written by Don Logan and published by Schiffer Milita Aviation History Books (ISBN 0-88740-800-1). Unfortunately for us, the T-38 is not a fighter or fighter-bom and doesn't have a gun, cannon or any sophisticated weapon system. Not even the attack version AT-38 wh has limited weapon delivery capabilities. Therefor no such pictures could be included for obvious reason

All the photos of the T-38A and AT-38 were taken by me during a few visits to Randolph AFB in San Anto TX, made possible by the following people: Ralph Monson of the Public Affairs Office and Ron "Bulldog" Bartel the 12LG/MAIB at Hangar 3. Thanks also to John Beattie of 12MAIB for arranging my special requests. I especi would like to thank Msgt Steve Smith for his patience while allowing me to measure the T-38 from probe tailpipe, fintip to ground, inch by inch. Only this way I could be certain to have not only the overall dimens correct, but also a near perfect "sit" of the aircraft. I also would like to thank my dear friend Maj Jim Rotra (USAF, Ret.) for lending me his Dash-1, it provided some valuable information. Thanks also to Frank Smith Luigino Caliaro for the many photos of Turkish T-38's, unfortunately we only had room to show two of th Finally, a thanks to David W. Aungst and R.Collins for sharing some of their pictures for this book.

Then I would like to thank a number of people who went to great lengths to provide me with all that needed on the newest Talon version, the T-38C. First and foremost I have to thank Thomas A. Hitzeman, C Systems Engineer, T-38C Flight Training Systems Program Office, Wright-Patterson AFB, OH, who, despite be involved in many urgent projects himself, found the time to get me all the info on Pacer Classic, the T-38 upgr program. Many of the T-38C photos have been provided by Captain Randall "Hacker" Haskin, Captain Anth "K-Bob" Sweeney and Captain S.James "Flash" Frickel, all instructor pilots of the 49 FTS, 479th FTG at Mc AFB, GA; Major Darren McTee, USAF Reserve; Bob Sanchez of Twobobs and finally Mike J. Idacavage who supp most of the NASA bird pictures. Their contribution made this book what it is, a very comprehensive study of T-38 Talon, in pictures. I hope you enjoy it!

Willy Peeters

Cover photos: Top: T-38A 66-403 and 68-096 of the 25th FTS "Shooters" stationed at Vance AFB, Oklahoma (photo by Richard Collins).
          Center: One of the white painted T-38A (65-395) at Vance AFB, Oklahoma (photo by Bob Sanchez).
          Bottom: T-38C 68-197 of the Black Knights at Moody AFB, Georgia (photo by Cpt. Randall "Hacker" Haskin).

© 2004 by DACO Publications
a DACO Products Division
Provinciestraat 8
2018 Antwerpen - Belgium

Printed in Belgium
ISBN: 90-806747-4-
Suggested Retail Pric
19.75 euro

Photo by Bob Sanchez

Photo by Mike Idacavage

p) Quite a number of aircraft have been adorned with the famous 9/11 "Let's Roll" emblem commemorating one of e saddest days in American history. The T-38 was no exception and the AT-38 above has it under the windscreen. The tail (insert) is taken from a Holloman AFB bird.

ottom) A Whiteman AFB T-38A awaiting its pilots on the Vance AFB ramp for the ride back home. This bird belongs to e 509th FTS, spotting their motto "Follow Us" on the tail fin. Of particular interest in this picture is the overall dark y finish instead of the two tone gray applied to most T-38's shown on the previous pages.

3

These two photos show the very peculiar shape of the T-38 Talon nose to good advantage, with the bottom side and the tip curving upwards.

Below a close-up of the UHF Communications antenna.

Photo by Bob Sanchez

Pitot tube used for testing, fitted to an Edwards AFB T-38.

Early markings as seen in the picture below were designed to enable to spot the aircraft from a mile away, where present schemes fit in the low-viz context. Today's avionics incorporate anti-collision devices rendering high viz markings obsolete.

Photo by Bob Sanchez

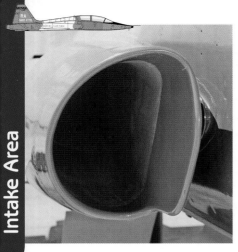

The T-38 has a very distinctive intake. Although narrow in height, the width allows adequate air to be ingested to supply the engines.

Note the opening between the fuselage and the intake splitter plate in the bottom left picture and the small splitter plate in the picture at right.

is T-38, despite being stripped of all paint except the temporary registration number on the aft fuselage, is nevertheless used for daily sorties from Randolph AFB, TX. It shows the various metals and composites used by Northrop.

Photo by R. C

CAUTION

NO STEP

Photo by Bob Sanchez

NO STEP

Photo by Bob Sanchez

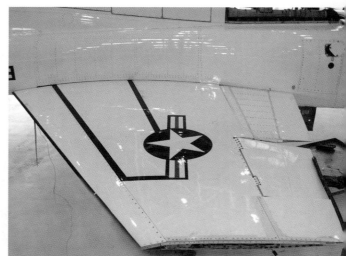

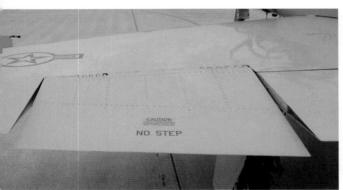

Photo by Bob Sanchez

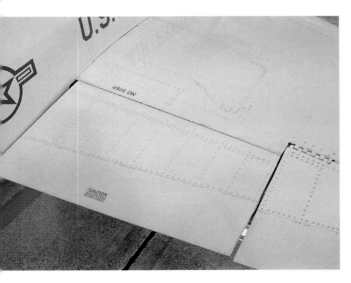

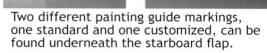

Photo by Bob Sanchez

Painted
BY DYNCORP
VAFB Oklahoma
TOPCOATED
20020221
Primer
MIL-P-23377G
Topcoat
MIL-C-85285

PMB: DYNCORP CAFB
DATE: 2003/04/01
PAINTED: RAYTHEON MAFB
DATE: 2003/05/02
X-IT PREKOTE
PRIMER MIL-P-23377G
TOPCOAT MIL-PRF-85285C

Photo by Bob Sanchez

Two different painting guide markings,
one standard and one customized, can be
found underneath the starboard flap.

Photo by Bob Sanchez

To prevent overheating of the engines, cooling ducts were installed on top of the aft empanage on both sides of the vertical tail. Note the shape of the spine tapering into the vertical tail.

The small round glass aft of the insignia is the hydraulic fluid indicator. The rectangular split door, marked by a light gray border, gives access to the engine oil tank.

The rear fuselage before and after a coat of paint has been applied. The different colors of the sections explain why some panels show a different shade even feauturing the same top coat. The little rectangular panel in front of the sp door hides the external AC power connection.

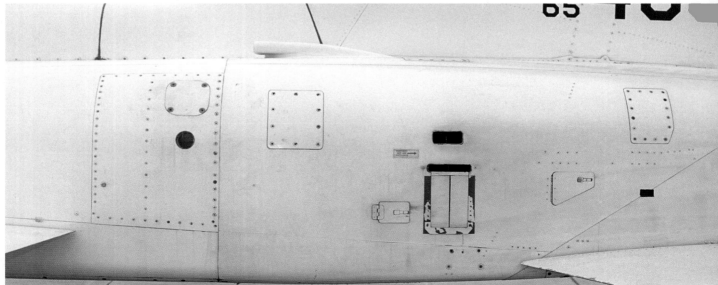

e empanage and its markings viewed from different
gles. Clearly seen is the single pivot point of the all-
vable horizontal tailplane, allowing better maneuve-
ility. Also note that the exhaust cover strap slings
und that exact pivot point and is secured by velcro.

Tail area with full color markings. Panel lines can be made out much clearer here. Note the single pivot point of the all-movable horizontal tail and the round position light between the bottom row of stars in the blue tail band.

Exhaust nozzles on the T-38 are hidden inside the tailpipes. They are shown in detail in the engine chapter. Note the unusual discoloring inside the tailpipes as well the fabric cover.

One of the few external differences between the T-38 and the AT-38 is the housing located at the bottom of the tail. Compare with the picture at bottom left.

Top: magnificent line-up of Talon Tales, sorry, tails with two "white feathered" birds joining the flock on the ramp at Vance AFB, Oklahoma on what seems a beautiful sunny day for flying. It is by no means a coincidence that most T-38 Fighter Training Squadrons are based in the most southern states of the USA.

Photo Richard

Unlike many other jets where the taxi light is mounted on the gear strut, the T-38's taxi light is retracted into the bottom fuselage, just in front of the main gear door.

Below: the large hole is the a/c heat exchanger outflow, the panel left gives access to the forward fuel cell drain valve while the little pipe at right is the a/c water drain.

19

Photo by Bob Sanchez

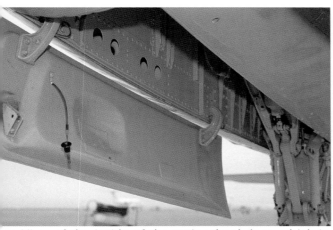

[Abo]ve: View of the inside of the main wheel door, which is [fu]lly closed after the gear strut is locked.

[Righ]t: View up into the nose gear well, looking forward. [At the f]ront in the right hand picture is the main door [retr]acting link, seen being disconnected here.

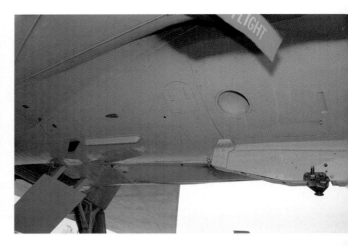

The aircraft's registration number can be found underneath the port air intake. Note the locator hole of the intake cover and the two small inspection panels.

The AT-38 underwent some slight changes to accept a belly pylon for limited weapons delivery although it is more commonly used to haul a travel pod.

Below and below left: travel pods with integral pylons standard for the T-38. Note the badge of the 7th Comb Training Squadron(CTS), the only F-117A training squad in the Air Force. The T-38 is used by the instructor pil "tailing" the single seat F-117.

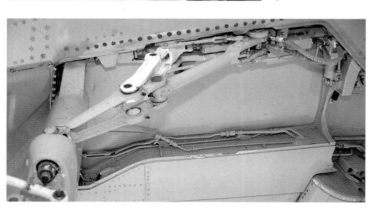

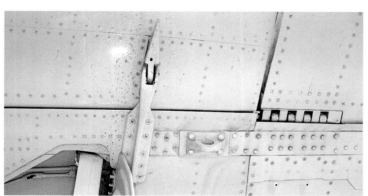

As can be seen below the front spars of both main wheel wells are identical and a mirror image of each other. Also clearly visible is that the dive brake segment has its own rear spar because this whole mid section of the fuselage belly is a single unit and can be removed for servicing. Pictures of this can be seen later in this book.

Photo Richard C

Top: A fine study of the flat underside, helping in locating the various sections described on this and the following page while showing to great advantage the "coke bottle" shape of the fuselage.

Next page, center photo: Clear view of the left and right engine bay and generator cooling vents. The yellow tubes are the left and right engine oil vents. The triangular blade antenna at top right is the IFF antenna as found only on the A model T-38. Note the relative moderate weathering because of the glossy paint coat.

The bottom fuselage has a distinctive concave shape at the end where titanium is used to absorb the heat from the exhausts.

The panels in front of the dual drain pipes at right are th External Air Connection access panels. See also bottom photo on next page.

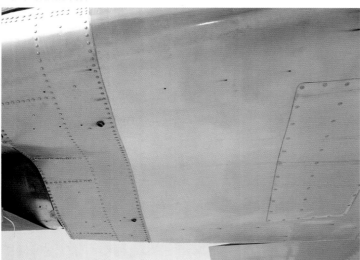

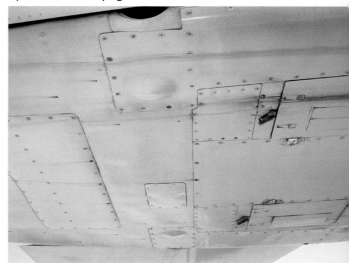

AOA
ALT
CLIMB
PERCENT RPM
NOZZLE
FUEL FLOW
UTILITY HYD PRESS
FLT CONT HYD PRESS
LDG TAXI LIGHT
START
LEFT
RIGHT
COMPASS
CHAN
MAIN
BOTH
ADF
VOL
TONE
MANUAL
PRESET
GUARD
SQUELCH
NAV
RAM DUMP
AUTO
MAN COLD
MAN HOT
CABIN PRESS
PITOT HEAT
CABIN TEMP
ENG ANTI-ICE
INCREASE
CANOPY DEFOG
CONTROL
SHOULDER HARNESS
LOCK
AUTO

MAIN INSTRUMENT PANEL
(Both Cockpits- Typical)

1 LANDING GEAR POSITION INDICATOR LIGHTS
2 ENGINE FIRE WARNING LIGHT
3 AOA INDEXER DIMMER
4 FLOODLIGHT
5 AOA INDICATOR
6 AIRSPEED / MACH INDICATOR
7 ATTITUDE DIRECTOR INDICATOR
8 ALTIMETER
9 MASTER CAUTION LIGHT
10 CANOPY WARNING LIGHT
11 ENGINE TACHOMETERS
12 EXHAUST GAS TEMPERATURE INDICATORS
13 CABIN ALTIMETER (Front cockpit only)
14 OIL PRESSURE INDICATORS
15 FUEL QUANTITY INDICATORS
16 NOZZLE POSITION INDICATORS
17 CARD FLIP
18 FUEL FLOW INDICATORS
19 HYDRAULIC PRESSURE INDICATORS
20 VERTICAL VELOCITY INDICATOR
21 HORIZONTAL SITUATION INDICATOR
22 MARKER BEACON LIGHT
23 NAVIGATION MODE SWITCH
24 STEERING MODE SWITCH
25 STANDBY ATTITUDE INDICATOR
26 CLOCK
27 ACCELEROMETER
28 DOWNLOCK OVERRIDE BUTTON
29 LANDING GEAR LEVER
30 LANDING GEAR WARNING SILENCE BUTTON

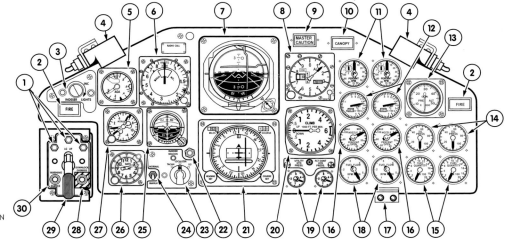

AUXILIARY PANEL LEFT
(Front Cockpit- Typical)

1 FUEL SHUTOFF SWITCHES
2 ENGINE START BUTTONS
3 LANDING GEAR RELEASE HANDLE
4 LANDING-TAXI LIGHT SWITCH
5 ADI FAST ERECT BUTTON
6 FLAP POSITION INDICATOR
7 INTERCOM SWITCHES
8 RADIO TRANSFER SWITCHES
9 COMM ANTENNA SWITCHES
10 COMPASS SWITCH

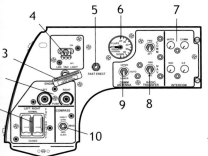

AUXILIARY PANEL RIGHT
(Front Cockpit- Typical)

1 CABINE PRESSURE SWITCH
2 CABIN AIR TEMPERATURE SWITCH
3 CABIN TEMP CONTROL KNOB
4 BOOST PUMP SWITCHES
5 FUEL/OXYGEN CHECK SWITCH
6 CANOPY JETTISON T-HANDLE
7 CABIN AIR INLET
8 BATTERY SWITCH
9 OXYGEN QUANTITY INDICATOR
10 GENERATOR SWITCHES
11 CROSSFEED SWITCH
12 CANOPY DEFOG KNOB
13 ENGINE ANTI-ICE SWITCH
14 PITOT HEAT SWITCH

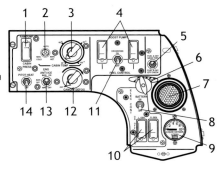

LEFT SIDE CONSOLE
(Front Cockpit- Typical)

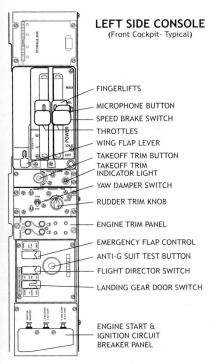

FINGERLIFTS
MICROPHONE BUTTON
SPEED BRAKE SWITCH
THROTTLES
WING FLAP LEVER
TAKEOFF TRIM BUTTON
TAKEOFF TRIM INDICATOR LIGHT
YAW DAMPER SWITCH
RUDDER TRIM KNOB
ENGINE TRIM PANEL
EMERGENCY FLAP CONTROL
ANTI-G SUIT TEST BUTTON
FLIGHT DIRECTOR SWITCH
LANDING GEAR DOOR SWITCH
ENGINE START & IGNITION CIRCUIT BREAKER PANEL

PEDESTAL
(Front Cockpit- Typical)

UHF COMMAND RADIO CONTROL PANEL
TACAN CONTROL PANEL
ILS CONTROL PANEL
RUDDER PEDAL ADJUSTMENT T-HANDLE
CIRCUIT BREAKER PANEL

RIGHT SIDE CONSOLE
(Front Cockpit- Typical)

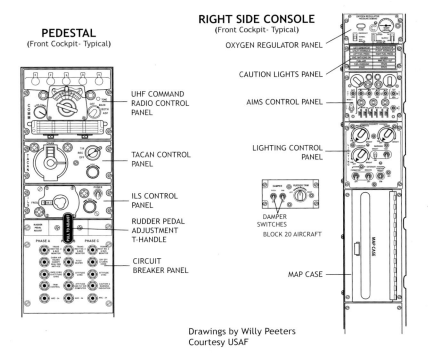

OXYGEN REGULATOR PANEL
CAUTION LIGHTS PANEL
AIMS CONTROL PANEL
LIGHTING CONTROL PANEL
DAMPER SWITCHES
BLOCK 20 AIRCRAFT
MAP CASE

Drawings by Willy Peeters
Courtesy USAF

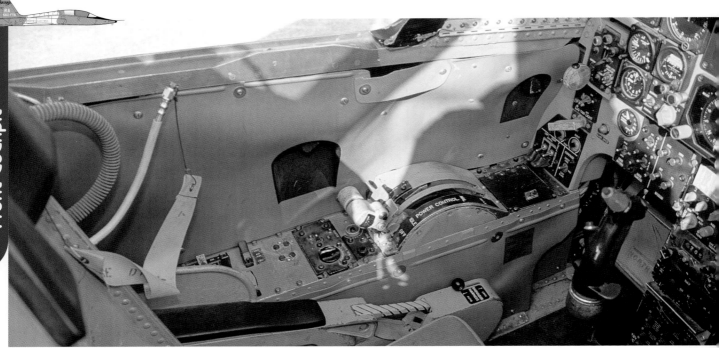

Since its development in the 1960's, the original cockpit layout has not changed much. The red tag indicates that the ejection seat safety pin is installed.

Each canopy can be jettisoned separately by adjusting the T-handle on the right auxilliary panel. From the outside both canopies can be fired in sequence with a one second interval by pulling the D-handle below the rescue panel. The canopy jettison system only functions properly when the canopies are closed and locked.

Photo Bob Sanchez

7 0 1 9 5
STU-P

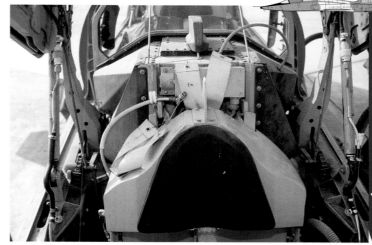

A window pane separates front and rear cockpits and allows individual pressurization of each cockpit. Also note the canopy piercer on top of the ejection seats' headrest.

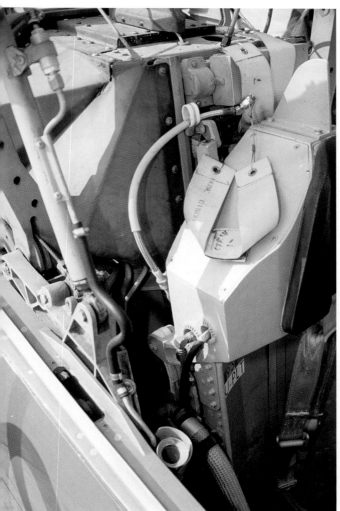

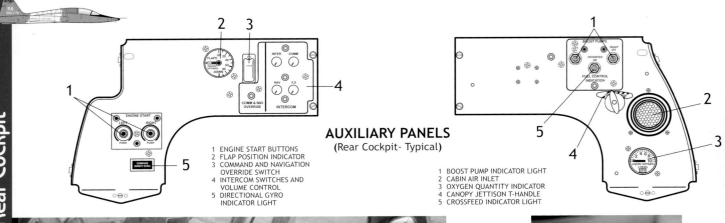

AUXILIARY PANELS
(Rear Cockpit- Typical)

1 ENGINE START BUTTONS
2 FLAP POSITION INDICATOR
3 COMMAND AND NAVIGATION
  OVERRIDE SWITCH
4 INTERCOM SWITCHES AND
  VOLUME CONTROL
5 DIRECTIONAL GYRO
  INDICATOR LIGHT

1 BOOST PUMP INDICATOR LIGHT
2 CABIN AIR INLET
3 OXYGEN QUANTITY INDICATOR
4 CANOPY JETTISON T-HANDLE
5 CROSSFEED INDICATOR LIGHT

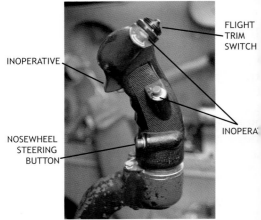

FLIGHT TRIM SWITCH

INOPERATIVE

INOPERAT

NOSEWHEEL STEERING BUTTON

Drawings by Willy Peeters
Courtesy USAF

CONSOLE PANELS
(Rear Cockpit- Typical)

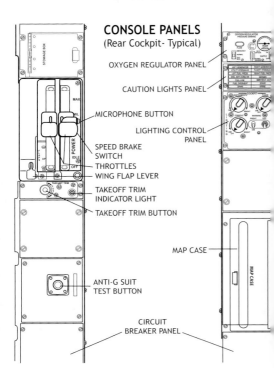

OXYGEN REGULATOR PANEL

CAUTION LIGHTS PANEL

MICROPHONE BUTTON

LIGHTING CONTROL PANEL

SPEED BRAKE SWITCH
THROTTLES
WING FLAP LEVER

TAKEOFF TRIM INDICATOR LIGHT

TAKEOFF TRIM BUTTON

MAP CASE

ANTI-G SUIT TEST BUTTON

CIRCUIT BREAKER PANEL

...ght that almost every
...AF pilot is all too
...miliar with because
...y spent countless
...rs acquiring their
...ng skills in this office.
...e layout is typical for
...960's design with the
...gine instruments (in
...l) to the right and
...flight and navigation
...truments on the left.
...e the reinforcement
...s on the inside of the
...ter frame and the
...her low position of the
...r view mirrors.

PEDESTAL

Rear Cockpit- Typical)

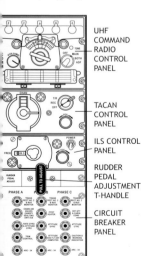

UHF
COMMAND
RADIO
CONTROL
PANEL

TACAN
CONTROL
PANEL

ILS CONTROL
PANEL

RUDDER
PEDAL
ADJUSTMENT
T-HANDLE

CIRCUIT
BREAKER
PANEL

...rawings by Willy Peeters
...ourtesy USAF

Clear view of the opposite side of the separation window pane between the two cockpits. Note the complex shape of the instrument coaming.

Replacing the canopy raising mechanism must be a mechanic's nightmare. No doubt that with today's technology the design would have been a lot simpler.

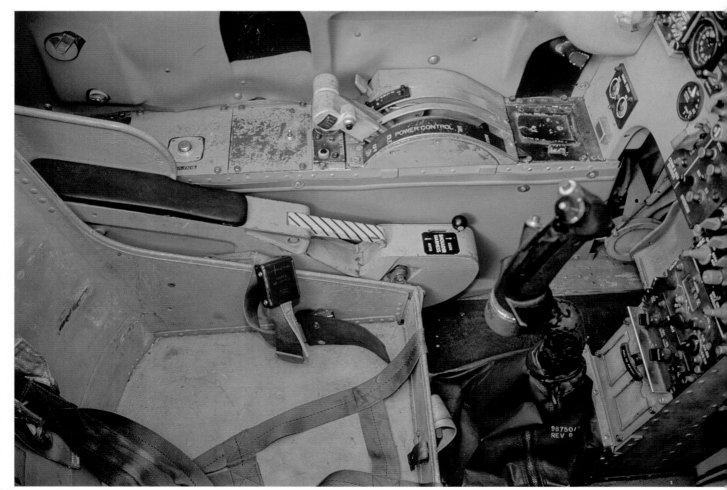

Photo Bob Sanchez

the label on the seat indicates the instructor pilot rides the back, while the front seat is marked similarly with tudent". Note that each seat also wears the aircraft's rial number. Although marked that way to assign each at to it's proper aircraft it allows easier identification in se of a crash as well.

e survival kit/seat cushion has been removed from the rcraft. Clearly visible in the top pictures is the yellow an/seat seperator strap below the shoulder harness.

ght: close-up of the very simple throttle quadrant. thin thumb reach are the speed brake switch and the crophone button.

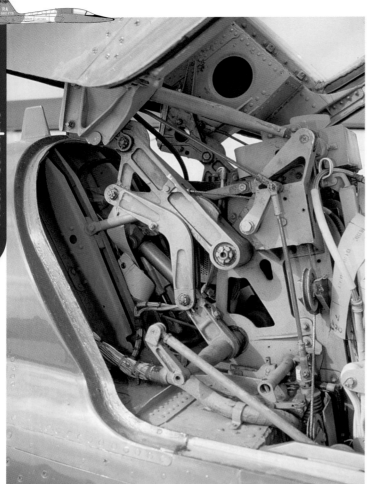

serve the more dedicated aircraft
thusiasts and advanced modelers we
luded these pictures of a stripped
ckpit in the maintenance hangar.
kages, rollers, cables and wiring
nstitute most of the earlier flight
ntrols, requiring many painstaking
urs of maintenance.
moved side wall panels reveal the
her narrow structural girders of the
ckpit area. Today's computer designed
craft differ significantly.
o clearly shown here is the ejection
t rocket catapult, secured with
ety pins, and the canopy actuator
pport mechanisms. Note the canopy
king lever at right.

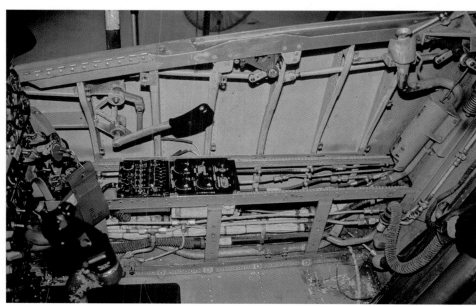

(Top) During major overhaul, the aircraft is practically stripped to check the various systems. A lot of lines run behind the side consoles.

(Bottom) Seat rails in the rear are braced differently because of the heavier canopy, requiring a more solid lifting mechanism.

canopy roller hook inspection panel (small round
ch) and the brake hydraulic reservoir just below the
board cockpit sill.

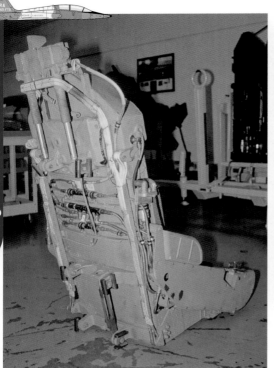
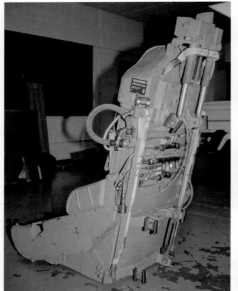
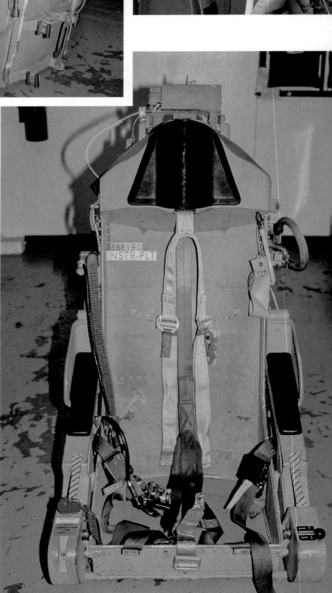
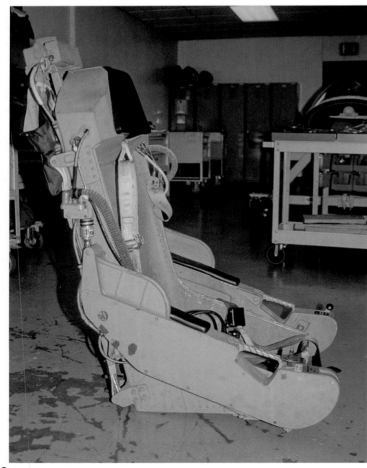

Rather than replacing the original ejection seat with a Martin Baker or ACESII seat, the original seat was improved with a drogue chute housing. The pilot still wears the parachute on his back and is being forced out of the seat by the man-seat separator, approximately 1 second after ejecting. The safety belt automatically opens. Future planned improvements to the T-38C will include an improved escape system.

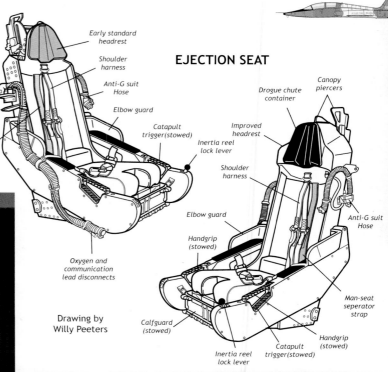

EJECTION SEAT

- Early standard headrest
- Shoulder harness
- Anti-G suit Hose
- Elbow guard
- Catapult trigger(stowed)
- Inertia reel lock lever
- Man-seat seperator strap
- Oxygen and communication lead disconnects

- Drogue chute container
- Canopy piercers
- Improved headrest
- Shoulder harness
- Anti-G suit Hose
- Elbow guard
- Handgrip (stowed)
- Man-seat seperator strap
- Handgrip (stowed)
- Catapult trigger(stowed)
- Inertia reel lock lever
- Calfguard (stowed)

Drawing by Willy Peeters

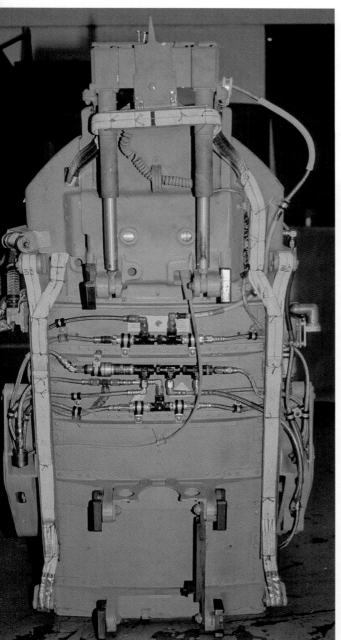

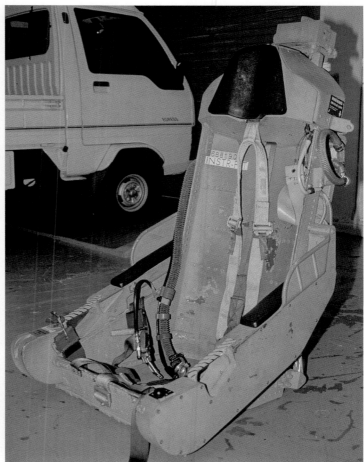

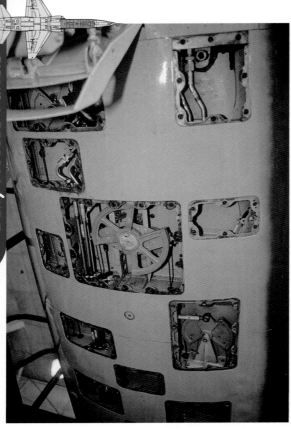

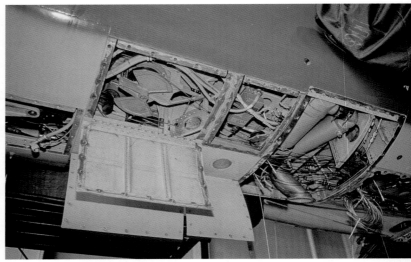

The bracket inside the housi[ng]
just aft of the beacon light i[s]
the horizontal stabilizer tens[ion]
regulator. The propeller-like
device is the right aileron
quadrant. The pipes to the ri[ght]
are air conditioning ducts.

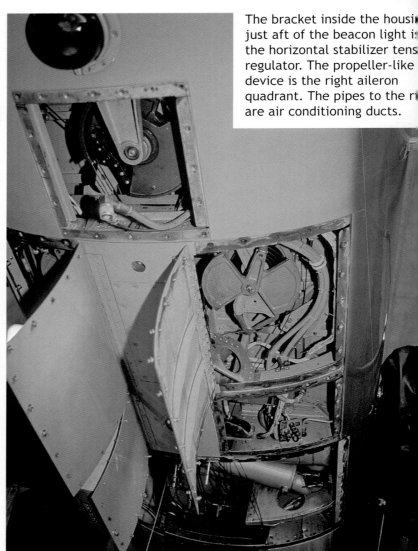

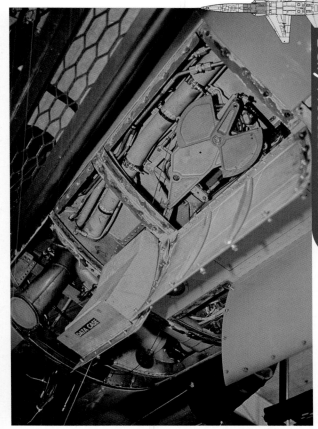

Again the right aileron quadrant is prominent in this view as well as the forms/data case. The green pipe is the conditioned air supply duct.

e silver piping and lector behind the ta case are the air nditioner inlet duct d water separator. e outlet in the bottom the picture is the a/c at exchanger outlet.

nterally located in the ture at right is the ward fuel cell access nel.

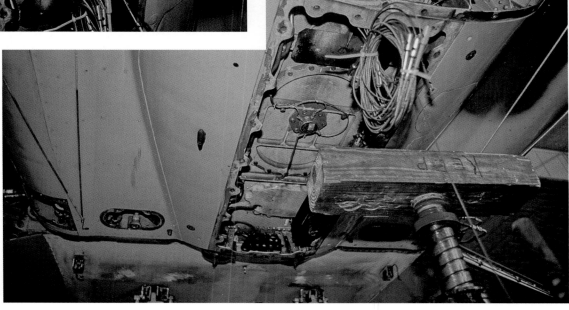

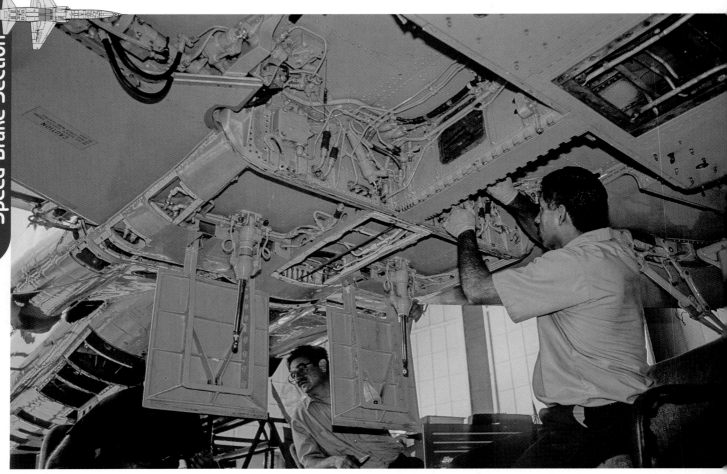

Three maintenance
crewmembers just
installed the very heavy
speed brake section
and are connecting
the numerous pipes
and feed lines.
A comprehensive
maintenance manual,
as well as experience
is indispensable for this
task.

The entire speed brake
housing section in front
of the main gear well
can be removed. Note
that the speed brake
actuators are attached
to the bottom fuselage.

lity hydraulic reservoir and pressure regulator below
large panel. The small panel at right covers the
gine inlet inspection hatch.

The same utility hydraulic reservoir on starboard side with
the starboard engine T5 Amplifier mounted on top of it.

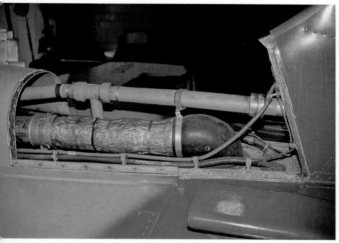

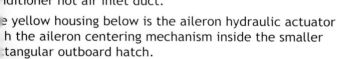

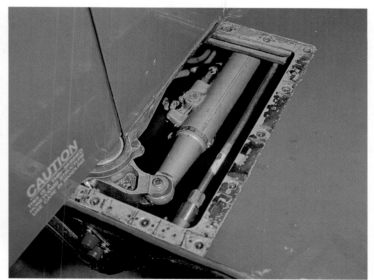

t of the spine can be removed to give access to the air
nditioner hot air inlet duct.

e yellow housing below is the aileron hydraulic actuator
h the aileron centering mechanism inside the smaller
tangular outboard hatch.

The rudder actuating rod can be accessed from a panel at
the top of the aft empanage at the tail root. The opposite
side is similar. Note the caution markings on the rudder.

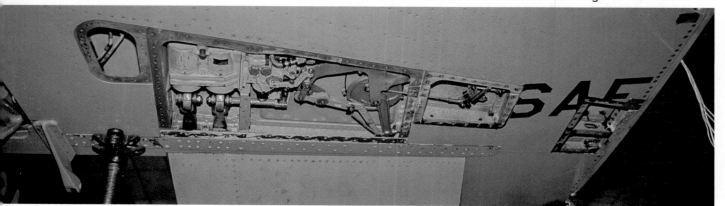

View looking
aft and into
the engine
compartment.

View looking
forward and
up into the
compartment
holding the end
part of the air
intake tunnels.

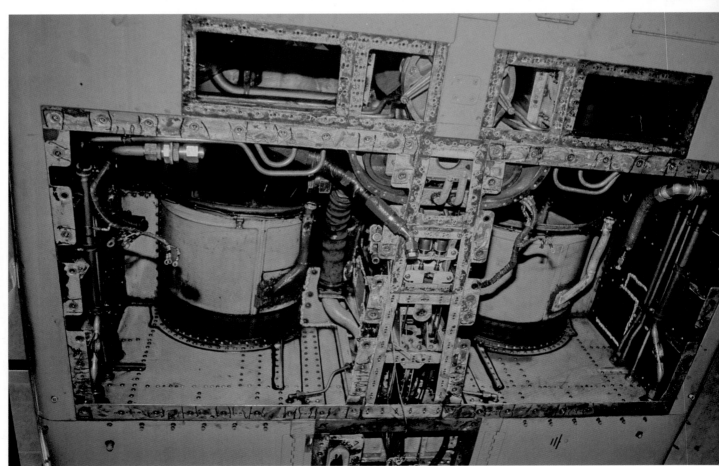

A Beale AFB T-38 (rear) hooked up next to a T-38 from Whiteman AFB at the Engine Test Facility, prior to some engine test runs. Note how carefully they have been lined up by the aid of guidance bars on the ground. Also note the "exhaust stack" on top of the building in the rear and the chain links to the main landing gear struts, holding the aircraft at bay while the enigine is being cranked up.

Two of these Pratt & Whitney J85-GE-5 engines power the T-38 Talon.

The J85-GE-5 is an eight-stage, axial flo[w] turbojet engine, providing approximate[ly] 2,050 pounds of thrust at MIL power and 2,900 pounds at full MAX power. Unlike most jet aircraft which have the variab[le] exhaust nozzles clearly visible, the T-38 nozzles are hidden within the jet exhau[st] pipes, but both bottom photos reveal these details. Note the nozzle actuator[s] on the side of the afterburner section. Each engine has a main fuel control system and an afterburner fuel control system.

This page pans the right side and botto[m] while the next page shows the left side[.]

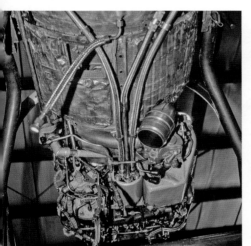

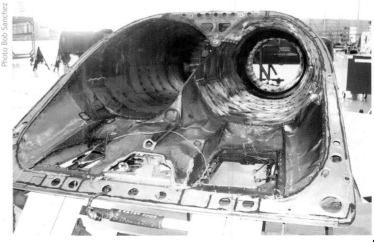

Photo Bob Sanchez

Photo Bob Sanchez

NASA has operated the T-38 for several years, both as instruction platform for their astronauts and as chase plane in their Shuttle Program. They are not included i the AUP program although some have been retrofitted with the larger intake (picture above) and the modified engine. Initial tests of the larger intake and improved engines for AUP were conducted on NASA T-38's.

NASA T-38's feature a different cockpit layout which ha no resemblence to either the T-38A or the T-38C, as ca be seen in the picture below.

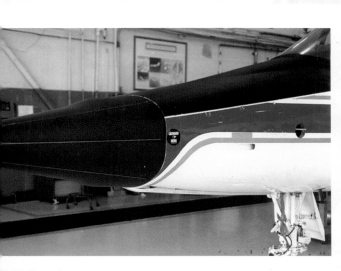

All photos on these pages were kindly provided by Mike Idacavage (unless otherwise indicated).

T-38C Talon
Pacer Classic Program

It is a great tribute to the Northrop engineers that the US Air Force decided to upgrade the venerable T-38, rather than replace it with a more modern design. Unfortunately, the Talon's avionics are so outdated that failures occur with increasing frequency and spare parts are becoming as rare as the Hope diamond. The 1950's era flight instruments of the T-38 A/B are technologically so inferior to the integrated avionics found in today's fighter and bomber aircraft that it is almost impossible for pilots to aquire the necessary avionics-related skills to make the transfer to follow-on bomber-fighter training.

Since the flight characteristics and performance of the T-38 remained well suited for the Air Force training purposes, it was decided to improve where the T-38 was lacking. Hence the Pacer Classic Program which, more than a specific upgrade, is an umbrella program to manage modifications as they become necessary and funded. The T-38 Program Office employs Contract Field Teams (CFTs) to perform field-level modifications, either in an individual unit, or centralized at one location as a Queen Bee operation. Currently, such an operation is hosted by Randolph AFB in Texas who performs two major transformations, the Avionics Upgrade Program (AUP) and the Propulsion Modernization Program (PMP). As soon as a T-38A or B model receives the AUP mods it is redesignated as a T-38C and is returned to operational service, in anticipation of the PMP modification.

The T-38 AVIONICS UPGRADE PROGRAM (AUP).

As part of the AUP, all of the navigation communications systems, plus the majority of the eng performance instrumentation are being replaced by mo state-of-the-art equipment:

- Global Positioning System (GPS)
- Internal Navigation System (INS)
- No-Drop Bombing System (NDBS)
- Radar Altimeter
- Traffic Collision Alert and Avoidance System (TCAS)
- Data Transfer System (DTS)
- Tactical Air Navigation (TACAN)
- HUD
- Multi-Function Display (MFD)
- Electronic Engine Display (EED)
- Up-Front Control Panel (UFCP)
- Hands-On Throttle and Stick (HOTAS)

The complete AUP modification adds approximatel pounds to the aircraft's weight. The T-38 AUP cont was initially awarded to MCDonnell-Douglas back in 1996 was to integrate "off-the-shelf" F-5 avionics designed by Israel Aircraft Industries (IAI) with integration enginee and testing by McDonnell-Douglas at its facilities in St. L

(continued on pa

reshly painted T-38C 71OG of the 25th FTS "Shooters" of the 71st FTW at Vance AFB, OK. The first phase of the upgrade (cockpit and tennas) has been completed but it still features the original intake and exhaust.

Photo by Darren McTee

The T-38C's most distinctive external feature, aside from the larger intakes, is the TCAS "wart". This anti-collision device will prove extremely useful in high volume traffic areas of operation, flying along with other TCAS-equipped aircraft.

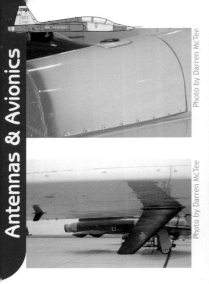

Photo by Darren McTee

Photo by Darren McTee

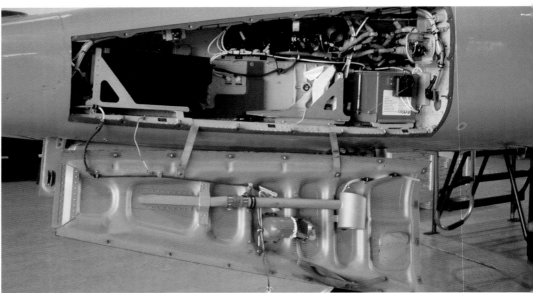

Photo by Darren McTee

Upgraded avionics in the T-38C are (left to right) a Mode S Transponder, TCAS computer (installed) and the red colored battery. An avionics cooling fan and moisture collector are mounted on the hatch. At left can be seen the new GPS antenna on the spine (top), the VHF Comm and TCAS antenna (middle) and DME & Mode Transponder blade next to the n wheel strut (bottom).

(continued from page 62)

When Boeing became the owner of McDonnell-Douglas they also acquired the T-38 AUP contract. However, during the development and the early test trials it became clear that such an upgrade would not meet operational requirements. A T-38 Cockpit Working Group, consisting of Boeing and IAI engineers, in collaboration with Air Force engineers and AETC Instructor Pilots revised the design to its current form.

In all, over 500 USAF T-38A/B aircraft are scheduled to receive the AUP upgrade, including those operated by the Air Combat Command (ACC) and the Air Force Flight Test Center (AFFTC) at Edwards AFB. As currently planned, the AUP is scheduled for completion in 2008 or soon thereafter and the T-38C is scheduled to fly well into 2020 when it will come close to logging it's 60th year of service. A remarkable achievement for any aircraft design.

Note the difference between the throttle quadrant in the front cockpit (left) and the rear cockpit (above). The finger lifts are not present in the rear cockpit.

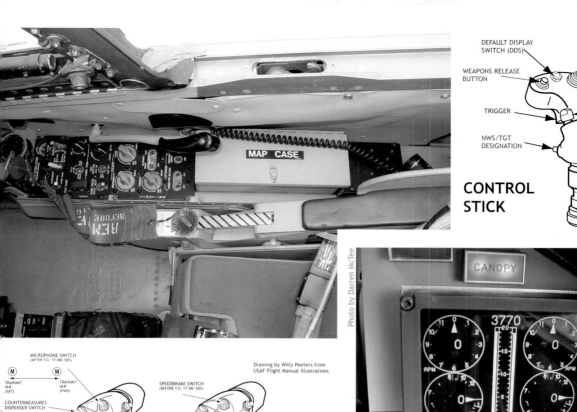

DEFAULT DISPLAY
SWITCH (DDS)

WEAPONS RELEASE
BUTTON

TRIM BUTTON

TRIGGER

MASTER
MODE
SWITCH

NWS/TGT
DESIGNATION

CONTROL
STICK

Ⓜ A/A (FWD) ← Ⓜ NAV (DN) → Ⓜ A/G (AFT)

Drawing by Willy Peeters from
USAF Flight Manual illustrations

Photo by Darren McTee

MICROPHONE SWITCH
(AFTER T.O. 1T-38C-505)

Ⓜ TRANSMIT VHF (AFT)   Ⓜ TRANSMIT UHF (FWD)

SPEEDBRAKE SWITCH
(BEFORE T.O. 1T-38C-505)

COUNTERMEASURES
DISPENSER SWITCH

MICROPHONE SWITCH
(BEFORE T.O. 1T-38C-505)

SPEEDBRAKE SWITCH
(AFTER T.O. 1T-38C-505)

Ⓜ Ⓢ Ⓜ

FRONT CPT Ⓢ Ⓢ

FINGER LIFTS
(FRONT CPT ONLY)

EXTEND (AFT)   HOLD (CTR)   RETRACT (FWD)

FRONT COCKPIT QUADRANT
(REAR COCKPIT SAME EXCEPT FOR THROTTLEGATE)

Drawing by Willy Peeters from
USAF Flight Manual illustrations

LEGEND
Ⓜ MOMENTARY- MUST BE HELD FOR CONTACT
Ⓢ SELECTED POSITION- CONTACT MAINTAINED IN SELECTED POSITION

THROTTLE

Photo by Darren McTee

Different imagery can be displayed on the Multi-Function Display (MFD) by just a push of a button.

MAIN INSTRUMENT PANEL
FRONT COCKPIT

1. ENGINE START CONTROL
2. COMM ANTENNA CONTROL
3. L/R FUEL SHUTOFF
4. EMERGENCY GEAR CONTROL
5. LANDING/TAXI LIGHT CONTROL
6. FLAP INDICATOR
7. AUDIO CONTROL PANEL
8. MASTER ARM SWITCH/CMD SWITCH
9. MARKER BEACON LIGHT
10. LANDING GEAR CONTROL
11. AOA INDEXER LIGHTS DIMMER
12. STBY VERTICAL VELOCITY INDICATOR
13. STBY ALTIMETER
14. STBY AIRSPEED INDICATOR
15. STBY ATTITUDE INDICATOR
16. MASTER CAUTION LIGHT
17. FIRE WARNING LIGHTS
18. AOA INDEXER LIGHTS
19. UP FRONT CONTROL PANEL(UFCP)
20. HEAD UP DISPLAY
21. HUD VIDEO CAMERA
22. CANOPY WARNING LIGHT
23. STANDBY MAGNETIC COMPASS
24. ELECTRONIC ENGINE DISPLAY (EED)
25. CABIN PRESSURE INDICATOR
26. NAV BACKUP CONTROL PANEL
27. UHF BACKUP CONTROL PANEL
28. HYDRAULIC PRESSURE INDICATORS
29. MULTI-FUNCTION DISPLAY(MFD)
30. WARNING/CAUTION/ADVISORY PANEL
31. FUEL CONTROLS
32. CANOPY JETTISON
33. ELECTRICAL CONTROLS
34. LOX QUANTITY INDICATOR
35. ECS VENT
36. DATA TRANSFER UNTI
37. RUDDER PEDAL ADJUST
38. CIRCUIT BREAKER PANEL

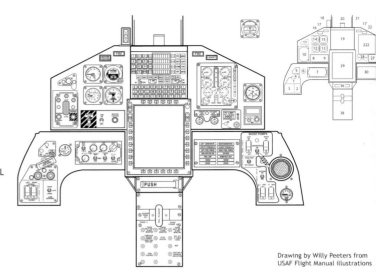

Drawing by Willy Peeters from
USAF Flight Manual illustrations

Photo by David W. Aungst

Photo by David W. Aungst

Photo by Darren McTee

Photo by David W. Aungst

One of the most prominent differences in the T-38C cockpit is the HUD and Up Front Control Panel (UFCP) as seen in the top three pictures.

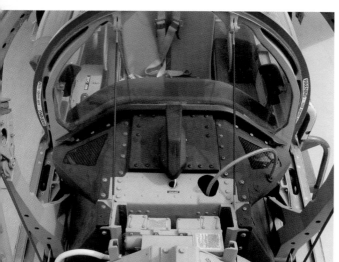

Structural differences are minor but the new instruments received an upgraded coaming with extra cooling screens on either side.

Photo by David W. Aungst

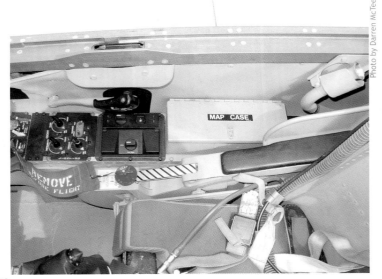

Photo by Darren McTee

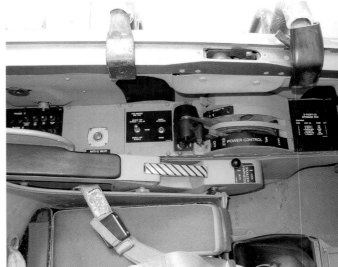

WARNING : KEEP HANDS CLEAR

RADIO CALL 630435

MAIN INSTRUMENT PANEL
REAR COCKPIT

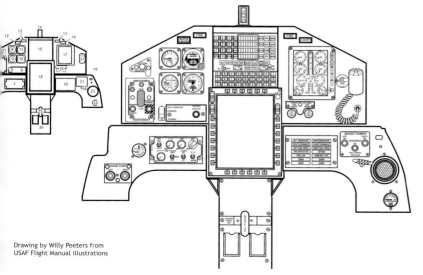

1. ENGINE START CONTROL
2. FLAP INDICATOR
3. AUDIO CONTROL PANEL
4. LANDING GEAR CONTROL
5. TAKE COMMAND SWITCH
6. MARKER BEACON LIGHT
7. AOA INDEXER LIGHTS DIMMER
8. STBY AIRSPEED INDICATOR
9. STBY VERTICAL VELOCITY
   INDICATOR
10. STBY ALTIMETER
11. STBY ATTITUDE INDICATOR
12. MASTER CAUTION LIGHT
13. FIRE WARNING LIGHTS

14. AOA INDEXER
15. UP FRONT CONTROL PANEL
16. CANOPY WARNING LIGHT
17. ELECTRONIC ENGINE DISPLAY (EED)
18. MULTI-FUNCTION DISPLAY (MFD)
19. HYDRAULIC PRESSURE INDICATORS
20. WARNING/CAUTION/ADVISORY PANEL
21. FUEL CONTROLS
22. CANOPY JETTISON
23. ECS VENT
24. LOX QUANTITY INDICATOR
25. RUDDER PEDAL ADJUST
26. CARD RETAINER PANEL
27. UTILITY LIGHT

Drawing by Willy Peeters from
USAF Flight Manual illustrations

71

Photo by Randall Haskin

The T-38 PROPULSION MODERNIZATION PROGRAM (PMP).

After receiving the APU modification each T-38C is returned to its unit until a later date when they are flown to the Queen Bee facility at Randolph AFB in San Antonio, Texas, where they are in line to receive the new GE J-85-5R. A 1997 study by the AETC proved that upgrading the

existing engine was the most cost effective method to obtain a reliable engine that was easier and cheaper to maintain. The PMP program ensures these improvements by replacing some internal engine components with more modern and reliable parts and by modifying the air inlet and exhaust nozzle ejector. Internal modifications include

Photo by Randall Haskin

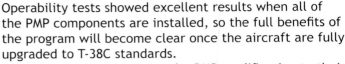

...mproved ignition system, turbine section improve-
...ts, a new combuster, replacing the existing stacked
...spacer compressor with a new spooled rotor
...mpressor and replacing several other components.
...itonally, the FS 332 Former and FS 362 Bulkhead will
...replaced as well, due to stress corrosion cracking,
...covered earlier.
...Changes made to the inlets will produce more thrust
...0% ground static thrust increase) while it reduces
...e-off roll by 12-15%, but it increased fuel consumption.
...However, in turn modifying the exhaust nozzle ejector
...roves both fuel consumption and engine performance.

Operability tests showed excellent results when all of
the PMP components are installed, so the full benefits of
the program will become clear once the aircraft are fully
upgraded to T-38C standards.

The first base to receive the PMP modification to their
T-38C's was Moody AFB, Georgia, while Columbus AFB,
Vance AFB, Randolph AFB, Laughlin AFB and Sheppard
AFB T-38's will all eventually receive the full upgrade
package when the Program will complete in 2008, as
scheduled.

Photo by Randall Haskin

Photo by Randall Haskin

GENERAL GE ELECTRIC
AIRCRAFT GAS TURBINE
U.S.A.F. MODEL   SPEC. NO.
J85-5R   E1024C
CONTRACT NO   SERIAL N
23-0714
FEDERAL STOCK NO.

The PMP modifications add another 143 pounds to the weight of the T-38. Although this is a significant increase, initial tests showed a static takeoff thrust increase by 19% in MAX power. The ground roll showed an improvement of 6.8% at 39°F to 19.9% at 82°F. Operability testing showed excellent results, so upgrading the existing J-85-5 engine was successful.

Photo by Randall Haskin

Most of the increase in fuel consumption caused by the large inlets was recovered by installing the new exhaust nozzle ejector. The first production exhaust nozzle ejectors were installed on NASA Talons. It should be noted that T-38 aircraft operated by NASA are not included in the Air Force Avionics Upgrade Program (AUP).

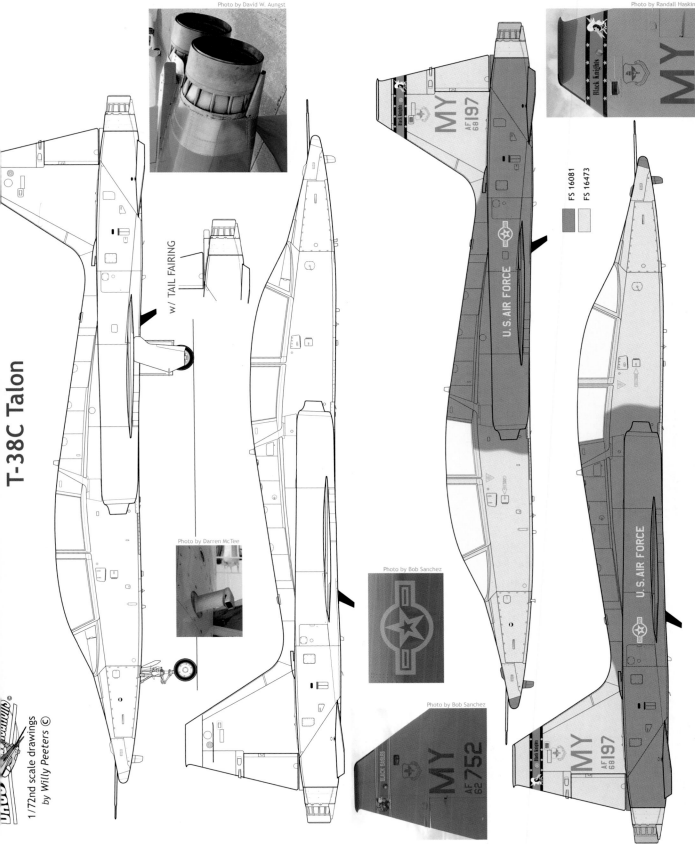

Photo by David W. Aungst

Photo by Randall Haskin

T-38C Talon

w/ TAIL FAIRING

Photo by Darren McTee

Photo by Bob Sanchez

Photo by Bob Sanchez

FS 16081
FS 16473

PAINT SCHEMES & COLOR REFERENCES

1/72nd scale drawings
by Willy Peeters ©

MY
AF 68 197

U.S. AIR FORCE

Black Knights

MY
AF 62 752

BLACK EAGLES

MY
AF 68 197

U.S. AIR FORCE

Black Knights

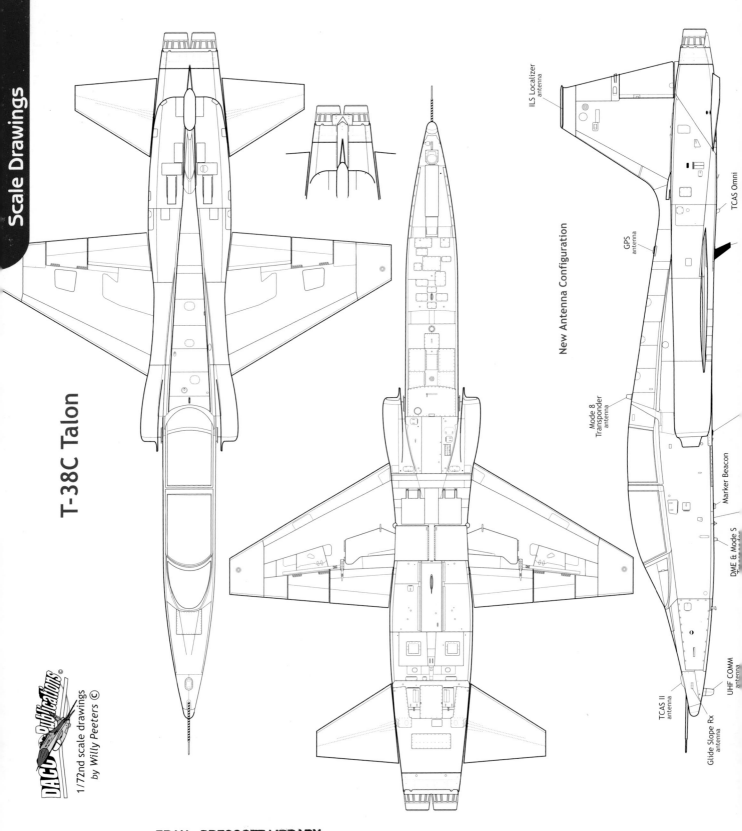

T-38C Talon

New Antenna Configuration

ILS Localizer antenna

TCAS Omni

GPS antenna

Mode 8 Transponder antenna

Marker Beacon

DME & Mode S

TCAS II antenna

UHF COMM antenna

Glide Slope Rx antenna

1/72nd scale drawings
by Willy Peeters ©

DACO Publications ®